Juno
Classroom Questions for Comparative Study

A SCENE BY SCENE GUIDE

Amy Farrell

SCENE BY SCENE
ENNISKERRY, IRELAND

Copyright © 2018 by Scene by Scene.

Without limiting the rights under copyright, this book is sold subject to the condition that it shall not, by way of trade or otherwise be lent, resold, hired out, reproduced, stored on or introduced into a retrieval system, or transmitted, in any form or by any means (electronic, mechanical, photocopying, recording or otherwise), or otherwise circulated, without the publisher's prior consent, in any form other than that in which it is published and without a similar condition, including this condition, being imposed on the subsequent publisher.

All rights reserved. No part of this publication may be recorded or transmitted in any form or by any means electronic, mechanical, photocopying, recording or otherwise without the proper consent of the publisher.

The publisher reserves the right to change, without notice, at any time, the specification of this product, whether by change of materials, colours, format, text revision or any other characteristic.

Scene by Scene
Wicklow, Ireland.
www.scenebyscene.ie

Juno Classroom Questions by Amy Farrell.
ISBN 978-1-910949-73-3

Contents

Part One   2
Cultural Context/Social Setting   3
Literary Genre   6
General Vision and Viewpoint   10
Relationships   13
Hero, Heroine, Villain   16

Part Two   18
Cultural Context/Social Setting   19
Literary Genre   23
General Vision and Viewpoint   27
Relationships   31
Hero, Heroine, Villain   35

Part Three   38
Cultural Context/Social Setting   40
Literary Genre   43
General Vision and Viewpoint   46
Relationships   49
Hero, Heroine, Villain   54

Part Four   56
Cultural Context/Social Setting   57
Literary Genre   60
General Vision and Viewpoint   64

Relationships	66
Hero, Heroine, Villain	70
Part Five	72
Cultural Context/Social Setting	73
Literary Genre	75
General Vision and Viewpoint	78
Relationships	82
Hero, Heroine, Villain	84
The Comparative Study	86
Cultural Context/Social Setting	87
Literary Genre	90
General Vision and Viewpoint	98
Theme/Issue: Relationships	104
Hero, Heroine, Villain	108
The Comparative Study: Comparing Texts	111

About This Book

This book is a companion guide for the Comparative Study of 'Juno', directed by Jason Reitman. Ideally it accompanies a second, detailed viewing and study of the film.

For the purposes of classroom study, I have divided the film into five parts. Each part contains an outline summary, a brief note on Cultural Context/Social Setting, Literary Genre, General Vision and Viewpoint, Relationships and Hero/Heroine/Villain, and a set of questions on Cultural Context/Social Setting, Literary Genre, General Vision and Viewpoint, Relationships and Hero/Heroine/Villain. The brief note is intended as a starting point for students, to provide something concrete for each mode that can be developed and built on by exploring the relevant mode-based questions in each part.

Towards the back of the book, there is a short note looking at each mode as a whole, across the entire film, and accompanying questions (please note, there may be some similarity with earlier questions to draw attention to key ideas).

Lastly, there is a section of questions on each mode, designed to prompt comparisons between 'Juno' and other Comparative Study texts.

Part One

Summary

From the opening up to 19.26 minutes, arriving at Leah's after the abortion clinic.

- Juno and Bleeker have sex.

- Juno discovers she is pregnant.

- Juno tells Leah that she is pregnant.

- Juno tells Bleeker that she is pregnant.

- Juno goes to the abortion clinic, but changes her mind and leaves without having an abortion.

Part One
Cultural Context/Social Setting

On first impressions, this is a world where teenagers enjoy a lot of freedom. Juno is free to have sex, discuss her pregnancy, and plan an abortion, without any parental interference.

Leah asks Juno which abortion clinic she will attend, assuming automatically that Juno will terminate her pregnancy. Similarly, Bleeker refers to their moms and teachers getting pregnant, suggesting motherhood is reserved for older, more responsible adults, and that pregnancy is not part of normal teenage life in this world.

There is a protester, a girl from school, outside the abortion clinic. Her presence suggests that abortion is an issue that teenagers care about. However, she is alone, this is not a huge issue in her community. Juno chats to her and listens to her point of view, there is no aggression or anger here. Perhaps this demonstrates that in Juno's world, teenagers have strong beliefs, and are capable of listening to one another and arriving at their own decisions.

Juno chooses to have her baby, rather than having a termination. This is a decision that she makes herself, without any pressure from anyone else. In this world, Juno is free to make this choice for herself. Although there is stigma attached to being a teenage mother, it is not such a burden as to make this an impossible choice for Juno.

Questions

1. What sort of place is this film set in, based on the opening sequence?

2. Are you surprised that Juno is discussing pregnancy tests with the store clerk?
   Does this tell you anything about these characters' attitudes or this place?

3. What does Juno's bedroom tell you about her world?

4. How does Leah (Juno's friend) react to learning that Juno is pregnant?
   What does she automatically assume?
   What does she talk to Juno about?

5. "That's what happens when our moms and teachers get pregnant."
   What does Bleeker's comment reveal about this world?
   What does it suggest about teenage pregnancy?

6. Whose responsibility is this unplanned pregnancy?
   What does this tell you about this world?
   Is Bleeker supportive of Juno?
   What does this tell you about this world?

7. What kind of girls do jocks secretly want, according to Juno?
   Does her insight here tell you anything about this world?

8. Describe Juno's family, based on what you have seen so far.

9. There is one protester outside the abortion clinic. What does her presence, and the exchange she has with Juno, tell you about this world?

10. What does Juno's experience in the abortion clinic tell you about this world?

11. Juno chooses not to have an abortion.
    Why, do you think, does she make this choice?
    Is this a difficult decision to make in this world?
    Give reasons for your answer.

Part One
Literary Genre

The film open with Juno and Bleeker having sex. This is the starting point of her pregnancy, which will be the basis of the story.

We then meet Juno as she discovers she is pregnant. There is humour in Juno's response to her positive pregnancy test (she calls the positive symbol "unholy"). This gives us an insight into Juno's character, showing that she is able to cope and is not overwhelmed by her situation.

The running team pass Juno, a visual reminder perhaps that Bleeker is on her mind.

Juno sets up a living room on Bleeker's lawn. This suggests that Juno is a quirky, off-beat character, and that Bleeker is well used to her and her humour.

Short flashbacks provide Juno's backstory and explain her relationship with her mother.

Juno's decision to have her baby is a major plot point and will fuel the action of the rest of the film.

Questions

1. What do you learn about these characters and this place from the film's opening sequence?
   Be specific in your answer.

2. Why, do you think, does the story begin where it does?

3. Comment on the stop-motion sequence.
   Does this cartoon-like sequence add anything to the story?
   How does it affect your expectations of the film?

4. What is the significance of the bottle of Sunny D?
   Is this well told?

5. Is Juno's chat with the store clerk funny? Why/why not?
   What does this add to the story?

6. Juno buys candy when she pays for the pregnancy test.
   What is the director telling us here?
   What does the candy noose and Juno's eating of it communicate to the audience?

7. Is Juno's pregnancy an interesting plot point?
   Give reasons for your answer.

8. How does Juno talking with Leah add to the story?

9. When we meet Bleeker, we see what he does before we see his face.
Why, do you think, does the director introduce Bleeker to us in this way?
Comment on the imagery when we meet Bleeker.

10. Juno has set up a living room on Bleeker's lawn.
What is your response to this?
How does this add to the story?

11. How does Juno's phonecall to the abortion clinic add to the story?
Does it reveal anything about her?

12. When Juno speaks about her mother, why don't we see her or her new family?
What is being communicated here?

13. What does Juno vomiting in the urn remind you of?
Is this effective storytelling, in your view?

14. How are short flashbacks used to good effect in this opening section?

15. Is Juno's chat with the abortion protester what you would expect in this situation?
What does this add to the story?

16. How do you know that Juno is uncomfortable in the abortion clinic?

17. Juno chooses not to have an abortion.
    What, if anything, does this add to your understanding of her character?
    What does this add to the storyline?

18. What are your impresssions of these characters after watching Part One?

19. How important is the soundtrack in telling this story?
    Use examples to support your point of view.

20. Do you think you will like this film?
    Give reasons for your answer.

Part One
General Vision and Viewpoint

From the beginning, Juno appears to be a positive, upbeat character. She openly discusses her pregnancy test with the store clerk, without fear or shame.

When Juno tells Bleeker she is pregnant, he asks what "we" should do, showing they are in it together. He looks scared to find himself in this situation, but does not react badly. In fact, neither one blames the other or finds fault.

When Juno suggests a termination, Bleeker agrees with her. This is a joint decision, between two characters who care about and support one another. Although a termination is a daunting prospect, the outlook is not hopeless, as Juno and Bleeker face it together. Juno is in control of her situation, showing her predicament in a less negative light.

Juno knows the abortion protester outside the clinic from school. This is not an aggressive, upsetting exchange. Juno listens to the other girl's point of view and thinks about it. Although this is a serious moment, it is not dark or upsetting.

Juno leaves the clinic, without having an abortion. This decision will have a big impact on Juno, and other characters in the film.

Questions

1. What is the song that plays during the stop-motion sequence about?
   How does the soundtrack impact on the mood of the opening sequence?

2. At first, how does Juno feel about being pregnant?
   Does she cope well with this development?

3. Juno's friend, Leah, thinks that Juno loves Bleeker. How does Juno respond to this idea?
   How does this impact on the story's mood?

4. How does Bleeker respond to the news that Juno is pregnant?
   How does he treat her here?
   How does this contribute to the general vision and viewpoint?

5. Bleeker is happy to support Juno's decision to have an abortion.
   Do you think she is happy with his response here?
   Give a reason for your answer.

6. How does Juno view having an abortion?
   Is her outlook positive or negative?

7. Is Juno's home a happy or a sad place, in your view?
   Give a reason for your answer.

8. Why does Juno not go through wiht the abortion, do you think?

   How does this affect the general vision and viewpoint?

Part One
Relationships

Juno and Bleeker have had sex, resulting in Juno getting pregnant, but they are not a couple. They are friends and have a good relationship. When she tells him she is pregnant, he asks what "we" should do, seeing it as something they will deal with together. He supports Juno's decision to have a termination.

Seeing Juno and Bleeker in science lab together gives us an insight into the dynamics of their relationship. They appear to get on very well. Juno copies Bleeker's work every week, and he is happy to let her. This may suggest that Juno has more power in their relationship, or that Bleeker wants to please her.

Juno and Leah have a strong, solid friendship. Juno tells her about being pregnant and they discuss her options together.

Questions

1. Based on what you have seen so far, describe Juno's friendship with Leah.

2. What reason does Juno give Leah for having sex with Bleeker?
   What is your response to this?

3. When did Juno decide to have sex with Bleeker?
   How does Leah respond to this?
   What is your response?

4. Does Juno admit to loving Bleeker?
   Can you explain this?

5. Comment on the scene where Juno tells Bleeker that she is pregnant.
   How does she break the news?
   How does he react?
   How do they treat one another here?
   What insight does this give you into their relationship?

6. Bleeker says Juno should do whatever she feels is best.
   What does this tell you about their relationship?

7. Whose idea was it to have sex?
   What does this suggest about their relationship?

8. What picture are you forming of Juno and Bleeker's relationship?

9. What do Juno and Bleeker's lab partners suggest about teenage relationships?
   Is this entirely serious, do you think?

10. What are your first impressions of Juno's relationships with her family?

11. Describe Juno and Bleeker's relationship as you see it.
    Are they just friends?
    Give reasons for your answer.

12. What impact will Juno's decision to continue with her pregnancy have on her relationships with her family, friends, etc. in your view?

Part One
Hero, Heroine, Villain

Juno is a quirky, independent, confident character. As the story unfolds, she is coming to terms with the fact that she is pregnant. She is not upset, but focuses on what she should do about being pregnant.

Juno makes a lot of jokes and adds humour to the start of the film, for example, setting up a room on Bleeker's lawn.

Juno decides to have her baby rather than having an abortion. She is willing to go through with the pregnancy and the judgement of others, showing her independent character.

Questions

1. What are your first impressions of Juno?
   Give reasons for your answer.

2. Who does Juno call when she discovers she is pregnant?
   What does their conversation tell you about how Juno is feeling?

3. Juno sets up a living room scene on Bleeker's lawn and waits for him to come out.
   What does this preparation tell you about her?

4. What does Juno's conversation with Bleeker about getting an abortion tell you about her?

5. Is Juno a good student?

6. Is Juno a quirky character?
   Does Juno seem like she is good fun?
   Give reasons for your answer.

7. What does Juno's story about the girl who took too many behavioural meds at once and jumped into a fountain at the mall, tell you about her?

8. Are you surprised by Juno's decision to have the baby?
   Give reasons for your answer.

Part Two

Summary

From 19.27 minutes up to 37.33 minutes, arriving at Leah's to leaving Vanessa and Mark's.

- Juno goes to Leah's house. She tells her she did not go through with the abortion and has decided to give the baby to someone who needs it.

- Juno and Leah find an adoption ad in the Pennysaver.

- Bleeker's mom tells him she does not approve of Juno.

- Juno breaks the news of her pregnancy to her dad and stepmom and tells them her plans to put the baby up for adoption.

- Juno and her dad go to meet Mark and Vanessa, the prospective adoptive parents, in their home.

Part Two
Cultural Context/Social Setting

When Juno tells Leah she is staying pregnant, Leah tells her to keep her voice down, as her mom does not know that they are sexually active. This suggests a division between the world of teenagers and their parents.

Leah points out the problems Juno will have if she stays pregnant, in particular, the issue of telling people that she is pregnant. She wonders if people will be mad and not let Juno graduate or go away for Spring Break.

Leah suggests looking at adoption ads in the Pennysaver, where adoption ads are readily available.

Bleeker's mother does not approve of Juno because she is "different". Her individuality is viewed negatively.

Mac (Juno's dad) and Bren (Juno's stepmom), though shocked, react calmly to the news of her pregnancy. This suggests that they will be supportive of her. It also suggests that in this world, teenage pregnancy, although by no means ideal, is something that her family can cope with and deal with.

Juno's family support, and the adoption ad, suggest that family is important in this world.

Vanessa's offer of compensation shows that she is prepared for Juno to expect payment in return for her baby. This suggests expectations of this nature may be widespread in this world.

Questions

1. What problems does Leah foresee if Juno stays pregnant?
   How does she think people will react?
   What does this tell you about this world?

2. Imagine if Juno lived in your town or community.
   How would news of her pregnancy be received?
   Is your town or community more supportive or more judgemental than Juno's?
   Give reasons for your answer.

3. Are you surprised that there are adoption ads in the Pennysaver?
   What does this add to your understanding of this world?

4. Why doesn't Bleeker's mother approve of Juno?
   What does this tell you about this world?

5. How do Juno's dad and stepmom react to her pregnancy?
   What does this tell you about this world?

6. Is Juno breaking the news of her pregnancy to her parents a big deal?
   What does this tell you about this world?

7. Comment on Juno's dad's attitude towards the prospective adoptive parents.
   What do his prejudices reveal?

8. Does Juno's stepmom have a good understanding of teenage life?
Give reasons for your answer.

9. "Anything but this."
What would have been preferable to pregnancy in Juno's parents' eyes?
Comment on this.

10. Why do Mark and Vanessa have an attorney present when they meet Juno?
What does this suggest about their outlook?

11. The attorney says Mark and Vanessa are willing to negotiate an 'open adoption'.
What does this mean?
Why, do you think, do Mark and Vanessa make this offer?

12. Vanessa asks Juno if she is looking for compensation from them.
What is Vanessa really asking here?
What does this tell you about this world?

13. What reason does Juno give for giving up her baby?
What does this tell you about her world and her place in it?

14. What does Mark and Vanessa's house tell you about them?

Part Two
Literary Genre

Juno tells Leah that she is going to stay pregnant. Leah points out the problems she will face, making the audience realise what Juno may go through.

There is humour when the girls read the Pennysaver ads, looking for suitable parents for Juno's baby.

Juno breaking the news of her pregnancy to her parents is a tense and exciting moment. Her adoption plan here is also a significant plot point.

Vanessa really wants the meeting with Juno to go well. Adopting a baby is clearly very important to her, and this is established from the moment we meet her. This desire to be a mother is a big driving force in her character.

Questions

1. Juno decides to stay pregnant.
   How significant a development is this?
   Give reasons for your answer.

2. How does Juno's decision to have the baby and her attitude to her pregnancy add to your understanding of her character?

3. What sort of family does Juno want to give her baby to?
   What does this tell you about her?

4. What is Juno's response to the picture of Mark and Vanessa in the Pennysaver?
   What is your response?
   How do you feel about this plan of Juno's?

5. We see Bleeker in his room, interrupted by his mother.
   What are we being shown in this scene?
   How does this help your understanding of Bleeker's character?
   Give reasons for your answer.

6. What builds tension in the scene where Juno tells her dad and stepmom that she is pregnant?

7. How do Juno's dad and stepmom react to the news of her pregnancy?
   What does this add to the story?

CLASSROOM QUESTIONS • 25

Is there humour in this scene?
If so, how does this add to the storytelling?

8. What do Vanessa's preparations before Juno and her dad arrive tell you about her?

9. What are your first impressions of Vanessa?

10. What are your first impressions of Mark?

11. What does Juno's meeting with Mark and Vanessa add to the story?

12. Is there humour in the scene where Juno meets Mark and Vanessa?
    What does this add to the story?

13. Is there tension in this scene? Why/why not?

14. How is Juno's youth shown in this scene with Mark and Vanessa?
    Why is the director drawing our attention to this?
    How does this add to your understanding of Juno's character?

15. What does Juno and Mark playing guitar together add to this scene?

16. Vanessa is worried that Juno will not go through with the adoption.
    Why might she feel this way?

What do her concerns add to your understanding of her character?

17. What is communicated through the characters' clothes and style in the scene where Juno and her dad meet Vanessa and Mark?

18. How is the innocence and naivity of Juno and Bleeker communicated in this section?

19. Is Juno a character that you like or can relate to? Give reasons for your answer.

Part Two
General Vision and Viewpoint

Juno hopes for the best regarding how people will react to her pregnancy. She is hopeful that everything will work out, despite the problems that may lie ahead. She is optimistic and kind, hoping to give the baby to someone who needs it.

Leah quickly moves on from the problems of Juno's pregnancy to the idea of adoption. Her attitude is also positive and forward-looking, not gloomy or pessimistic.

Juno's dad and stepmom are taken aback by the news of her pregnancy. However, they take the news quite calmly and focus on what will happen next. There is no anger here, they will continue to love and support Juno as before. This is a positive portrayal of family life, suggesting a bright outlook for Juno's future.

Juno's dad quickly moves on to the idea of adoption. His forward-looking stance is positive.

Bren, Juno's stepmom, accepts Juno's pregnancy and makes plans to deal with it. She does not blame anyone, or talk about the negatives. Her positive reaction adds to the general vision and viewpoint, suggesting optimism and supportive relationships. Significantly, Juno's pregnancy has not damaged her relationships with her parents.

Juno tells Vanessa and Mark that she is positive that she will go through with the adoption. She believes that they will provide a good home for her baby. This is a very positive and determined way to approach adoption.

Mark and Vanessa are a nice couple. They are welcoming and sincere, and capable of providing well for the baby. This suggests that Juno is making a good decision, and that the baby will have a promising future, ideas that show a positive general vision and viewpoint.

Questions

1. Juno decides not to have an abortion, but to stay pregnant.
   Does she have a plan here?
   Is her outlook hopeful or hopeless?

2. Juno wants to give her baby to someone who "needs it".
   Comment on Juno's decision here.
   Is this a kind or selfish act on Juno's part?

3. Leah sees lots of problems with Juno staying pregnant.
   Does she manage to convince Juno that it is a bad idea?
   Is Juno optimistic or doubtful?

4. Leah advises Juno to look at adoption ads.
   Is this good advice?
   Is Leah's outlook optimistic or pessimistic?

5. Describe the mood at this point.

6. How do Juno's dad and stepmom react to the news of her pregnancy?
   Overall, is this a good or bad reaction?
   Give reasons for your answer.

7. "Somebody else is going to find a precious blessing from Jesus in this garbage dump of a situation."
   Does Bren (Juno's stepmom) sum up the situation accurately here?
   Is her outlook positive or negative?

8. What is the 'feel' of the film up to this point?
   Describe what you mean, including examples.

9. Why, do you think, doesn't Juno want an 'open adoption'?
   How does this make you feel?
   Do you understand what makes her feel this way?

10. How does Vanessa's unfulfilled desire to be a mother affect the mood of this scene?

11. Juno does not want any money in exchange for her baby.
    What does this tell you about her motivation?
    How does this contribute to the film's outlook?

12. What does Juno want for her baby?
    How does this contribute to the film's outlook?

13. Vanessa tells Juno that she is doing something beautiful and selfless for them.
    How does this contribute to the film's outlook?

14. Is Juno overwhelmed by her pregnancy?
    Is she coping well?
    What does this suggest about life?

15. Is Juno's visit to Mark and Vanessa a positive or negative development?
    Give reasons for your answer.

Part Two
Relationships

Leah is a good friend to Juno. She listens to her and supports her as Juno comes to terms with her pregnancy, and is even there when Juno breaks the news to her dad and stepmom.

Juno's dad is surprised that Bleeker is the father of Juno's unborn baby. Juno jumps to Bleeker's defence here, showing how she cares about and values him.

Juno's dad and stepmom accept the news of her pregnancy without anger or upset. Although they are not happy about it, it does not change how they feel about Juno, they will continue to love and support her. This is a very positive portrayal of family relationships.

Mark and Vanessa are very warm and welcoming towards Juno and her father. Juno and Mark hit it off from the very start as they share an interest in music.

Questions

1. Is Leah a good friend to Juno when Juno tells her she plans to stay pregnant?
   Give reasons for your answer.

2. What plans did Juno and Bleeker have for Spring Break?
   What does this tell you?

3. What is Bleeker doing in his room?
   What does this suggest?

4. Juno has signed herself "Your Best Friend" in Bleeker's yearbook.
   Are they best friends, do you think?

5. What are your first impressions of Bleeker's relationship with his mother?

6. Leah is with Juno when Juno breaks the news of her pregnancy to her dad and stepmom.
   What does this suggest about their friendship?

7. How well do Juno's dad and stepmom take the news of Juno's pregnancy?
   How do they treat her here?

8. Is Juno very honest with her parents?
   What does this tell you about their relationship?

9. Juno's dad is surprised that the father of her baby is Paulie Bleeker.

How does Juno react to her dad's surprise?
What does this tell you about how she feels about Bleeker?

10. Juno's dad insists that he will go to meet the adoption couple with her.
    Is he supportive or interfering here?

11. How does Juno's dad show that he is not happy about her pregnancy?

12. Does Bren blame Mac for Juno's pregnancy?
    What does Bren and Mac's conversation when the girls leave the room reveal about their relationship?

13. Bren says that having sex was Juno's idea, not Bleeker's.
    How does this add to your view of Juno and Bleeker's relationship?

14. Does Juno have a good relationship with her dad and stepmom, based on what you have seen so far?
    Give reasons for your answer.

15. How well do Juno and her dad get on with Mark and Vanessa when they meet them?

16. Do Mark and Vanessa get on well?
    Use examples to support your point of view.

17. What interest do Mark and Juno share?
    Do they get on well together?
    Give reasons for your answer.

18. Were Juno and Bleeker a proper couple before she got pregnant?
How does her pregnancy complicate their relationship? Be specific in your answer.

Part Two
Hero, Heroine, Villain

Juno is very honest when she breaks the news of her pregnancy to her dad and stepmom. She is worried how they will respond, but she hides nothing from them.

Juno shows maturity and independence with her decision to have her baby adopted. She has made this choice herself, for her own reasons, and is committed to seeing it through.

When meeting Mark and Vanessa, Juno does not pretend to be someone she is not. She makes her usual jokes and remarks and is very much herself.

She does not want payment in exchange for her baby. This suggests she sincerely wants her baby to be happy with a good family.

Questions

1. What reasons does Juno give for staying pregnant?

2. What attitude does Juno have towards continuing with her pregnancy?

3. "I don't really know what kind of girl I am."
   What does Juno's line here reveal about her?
   Do you think this is often the case for sixteen year olds?

4. What do Bren and Mac make of Juno's pregnancy?

5. How do Bren and Mac view Juno?

6. "Mac, come on, you know it wasn't his idea."
   What do Bren's words here tell you about Juno?

7. How does Juno act when she meets Mark and Vanessa for the first time?
   What does this tell you about her?

8. What concerns does Juno mention regarding pregnancy?
   What does this tell you about her?

9. Juno does not want to be paid for giving her baby up for adoption.
   What does this tell you about her and her reasons for giving her baby up for adoption?

10. What does Juno do in Mark and Vanessa's bathroom?
    Does this tell you anything about her?

11. Is Juno a typical sixteen year old?
    Give reasons for your answer.

12. What good points/positives can you identify in Juno's character so far?

13. What bad points/negatives can you identify in Juno's character so far?

14. Is Juno an easy character to like?
    Give reasons for your answer.

15. Is Juno an easy character to relate to?
    Give reasons for your answer.

Part Three

Summary

From 37.34 minutes up to 59.44 minutes, Bleeker and Vijay at the track to Vanessa talking to Juno's bump.

- Bleeker chats to Vijay about Juno being pregnant while running at the track.

- Juno goes for her ultrasound with Bren and Leah.

- Juno calls to Mark and Vanessa's with the ultrasound picture.

- Bren tells Juno that she cannot drop in on Mark and Vanessa. Juno disagrees with her.

- Juno visits Bleeker. He suggests that they go out again, after the pregnancy. Juno wonders if they were ever together. She suggests that Bleeker should go out with Katrina De Voort.

- Vanessa struggles to pick the perfect shade of paint for the baby's room.

- Juno and Leah see Vanessa at the mall.

Part Three
Cultural Context/Social Setting

The ultrasound technician disapproves of Juno's pregnancy. At first she assumes Mark and Vanessa are friends from school, and is relieved to hear they will be adopting Juno's baby, viewing teenage mothers as unfit parents. Bren challenges the ultrasound technician's disapproving attitude.

Bren warns Juno that her dropping in on Mark is inappropriate. She tells Juno that Mark is a married man, and as such, there are boundaries that she should observe. Juno challenges this attitude, feeling that in her unique situation, she can choose to be friends with him if she wishes.

Juno visits Bleeker and assures him that her dad and Bren will not say anything to his family about her being pregnant. Bleeker is relieved to hear this. It seems that his parents are unaware that he is the father of Juno's baby, and that it will stay this way.

Questions

1. "Did you hear, Juno McGuff's pregnant...Like our moms and teachers."
   What does Vijay's comment reveal to you about his view of pregnancy?

2. Why, do you think, does the school secretary stare at Juno's bump?

3. "They're the adoptive parents."
   "Oh, well, thank goodness for that."
   Comment on the ultrasound technician's attitude here.
   Do you think this is a commonly held belief?
   Give reasons for your answer.

4. Why does Mark think it is unlikely that they will have a baby shower?
   What does this tell you about their situation and how their family and friends feel about it?

5. According to Bren, why can't Juno drop in on Mark and Vanessa?
   What is Juno's outlook?
   Do you agree with Juno or Bren here?
   Give reasons for your answer.

6. Juno jokes to Vanessa that at school she is the "cautionary whale".
   What does this mean?

What insight does this give you into what life is like for Juno at present?

7. Juno tells Bleeker that her parents will not tell his parents about him getting her pregnant, something that brings him great relief.
Are you surprised that Bleeker's parents do not know that he is the father of Juno's baby?
Does this tell you anything about this world?
Are Juno and Bleeker treated the same way by their peers and the adults around them because of Juno's pregnancy? Use examples to support your view.

8. What attitudes and values have you noticed in what you have seen so far?

Part Three
Literary Genre

Snow has fallen, showing that time is moving on.

Notice the difference in Juno and Bleeker's bedrooms and what this suggests about their characters. Juno's room is an eclectic mix, while Bleeker's still resembles the room of a younger boy, with his racing car bed and astronaut decorations.

In the scene in Bleeker's room it is clear that he cares about Juno. He says she is beautiful, and suggests that they could get back together. This romantic moment does not develop however, as Juno questions if they were ever together, and suggests that he should go out with another girl, Katrina De Voort. This leaves the question of a romance between them unresolved.

Being a mother is very important to Vanessa. We see this in her attention to detail and exhaustive preparations for the baby's arrival. She agonises over the correct shade of yellow for the baby's room. Mark does not seem to share her enthusiasm, telling her that there is still plenty of time.

Meeting Vanessa in the mall, Juno sees how committed to motherhood she is. Talking to Juno's bump, it is clear how much she wants this baby, something that makes Juno happy.

Questions

1. Why are the snowfall and the 'Winter' heading significant?

2. Is there humour in Vijay's chat with Bleeker? Why/why not?

3. How does 'I'm sticking with you' playing in the background add to the story here?

4. What makes Bren insult the ultrasound technician?
   How does this add to her character?
   Are you glad she spoke up for Juno here? Why/why not?

5. We see Juno lying on her bed, looking at the ultrasound picture.
   What, do you think, is she thinking?

6. Why does Juno go to Mark and Vanessa's?

7. How does Mark react to Juno turning up like this?

8. What are your impressions of Mark so far?
   Give reasons for your answer.

9. How does Mark respond to the ultrasound picture?

10. "You are something else."
    Comment on Mark and Juno's relationship, as you see it.
    How do you expect this relationship to develop?

11. Juno goes to see Bleeker.
    What does this scene add to the story?

12. What does Mark and Vanessa choosing paint add to the story?
    What insight does it give you into how each of these characters is feeling?

13. Does humour play a big role in this film?
    Explain your point of view.

Part Three
General Vision and Viewpoint

In the ultrasound scene, we see both the positive and negative sides of life. Leah and Bren are with Juno, and they are happy to see the pictures of her baby on the screen.

The ultrasound technician's nasty remarks show the negative side of human nature. She is quick to jump to conclusions about Juno and her ability to be a parent, thinking the worst of her.

However, the way that Bren immediately jumps to Juno's defence shows how she loves and values her stepdaughter, a very warm and positive gesture.

When Juno tells Bleeker about the private adoption, his first question is to ask what the adoptive parents are like. Although he is removed from the decision-making, he cares about Juno and what will happen to the baby.

Becoming a mother is very important to Vanessa. We see her trying to pick the perfect paint for the baby's room, and happily playing with a child in the mall. Her enthusiasm about becoming a mother creates a sense of potential and optimism in the film. It also shows that Juno has made the right decision and is bringing happiness into Vanessa's life.

Questions

1. How, do you think, does Bleeker feel about Juno?
   Is he able to express how he feels?
   How does this make you feel?

2. Bleeker asks if he should go to the ultrasound.
   How does this affect the general vision and viewpoint?

3. How do Juno, Leah and Bren respond to seeing the baby on the screen?
   Is this a positive or negative moment?

4. Bren insults the ultrasound technician when she suggests that Juno would not make a good parent.
   How do Bren's actions here influence the general vision and viewpoint of the scene?

5. Why won't Vanessa have a baby shower?
   How does this make you feel?

6. How does Bren feel about Juno visiting Mark?
   What is going on here?
   How does this make you feel?

7. "I always think you're cute."
   How do Bleeker's words to Juno make you feel?

8. "We could always get back together too."
   How does Juno respond to Bleeker's suggestion that they could get back together?
   How does this make you feel?

9. Why does Juno smile when she sees Vanessa and the little girl in the mall?

10. How do Vanessa's hopes of being a mother make you feel?

11. How does humour affect the general vision and viewpoint of this section?

12. Where do you see happiness in this section?

13. Where do you see sadness in this section?

Part Three
Relationships

Bleeker invites Juno to the movies with him and some friends, but she declines. He offers to go to the ultrasound with her, but she tells him to go to the movies instead. She says she will call by later. Although they have not been spending a lot of time together, they get on well.

Bren stands up for Juno when the ultrasound technician says that teenage mothers raise their children in poisonous environments. Bren cares about Juno and is not happy to have her spoken to this way.

Juno and Mark get on well together, sharing interests in music and horror films. She enjoys spending time with him and describes him as 'awesome' to Bleeker and 'cool' to Bren. Mark seems happiest discussing music, rather than the baby, with Juno.

Bren does not approve of Juno visiting Mark, viewing it as overstepping boundaries to visit a married man like this. Juno does not take Bren's concerns seriously, arguing that she can be friends with someone who is married if she wants to. Bren seems concerned that Juno's relationship with Mark may develop inappropriately.

Bleeker asks her if it is normal to visit adoptive parents and spend time with them like this, something that Juno realises is probably not the case.

Juno worries that Bleeker will no longer find her attractive when she gets bigger. This is the first time she has expressed any concerns like this. He reassures her, telling her that he always thinks she is cute. Bleeker appears to be in love with Juno, but confusingly, she encourages him to go out with another girl, Katrina De Voort.

Questions

1. Vijay chats to Bleeker about Juno being pregnant. Bleeker says that he doesn't really know too much about it.
   What does this suggest to you about him and Juno?

2. Bleeker offers to go to the ultrasound with Juno.
   Why does he do this, do you think?
   Why doesn't he go with her?

3. Describe Juno and Bleeker's relationship as you see it at this point.

4. Who goes to the ultrasound with Juno?
   Why have they gone with her?
   Does Juno have supportive family and friends?

5. Juno wants to keep the baby's sex a surprise for Vanessa and Mark.
   What does this tell you about how Juno feels about them?

6. What does the ultrasound scene add to your understanding of Juno and Bren's relationship?

7. Do Juno and Mark get on well together?
   Use examples to support your viewpoint.

8. Is Juno impressed by Mark?
   Explain your point of view.

9. What exactly, is Juno and Mark's relationship?
How do you feel about Juno and Mark's relationship?
Give reasons for your answer.

10. "There's Vanessa, you'd better go."
What picture of Mark and Vanessa's relationship are you forming?

11. How does Bren react to hearing that Juno drove over to Mark's and spent time with him?
Does Bren trust Juno?
What is going on here?

12. Why does Bren discourage Juno from visiting Mark, do you think?

13. Bren says she has sacrificed a lot for Juno.
Is this true, do you think?
Give reasons for your answer.

14. Is Bleeker's mom happy that Juno calls over?
How do you know?

15. Why has Juno called over to Bleeker's?

16. Does Bleeker care about Juno?
Give reasons for your answer.

17. Does Juno care about Bleeker?
Give reasons for your answer.

18. What does this scene in Bleeker's bedroom tell you about their relationship?

19. Why does Juno mention Katrina De Voort? What is she doing here?

20. "I think it's too early to paint."
    Do Mark and Vanessa share the same outlook about the adoption, do you think?
    Give reasons for your answer.

21. How, do you think, does Juno feel about Vanessa as this section ends?
    What makes her feel this way?

Part Three
Hero, Heroine, Villain

Juno is not affected by seeing her baby onscreen, or by the ultrasound technician's derogatory comments. She appears content with her decision and unconcerned by what others think.

When Bren warns Juno that visiting Mark is inappropriate, Juno stands her ground, insisting that she can have married friends if she wants to.

At Bleeker's, Juno worries that he will no longer find her cute when she gets bigger. When he reasuures her, and suggests that they get back together, she questions whether they ever were together, and encourages him to go out with another girl, Katrina De Voort. Perhaps Juno cannot see past her pregnancy at this point, or does not realise what she wants from Bleeker at this stage.

Questions

1. Does Juno care about Bleeker, do you think?
   Give reasons for your answer.

2. Is Juno bothered that people may disapprove of her pregnancy?
   Give reasons for your answer.
   How does this add to your understanding of her character?

3. How does Juno's bedroom reflect her personality and add to your understanding of her personality?

4. How does Juno respond to learning that Mark is a composer?
   Why does she call him a sell-out?
   Is she easily impressed, do you think?

5. Bren tells Juno that she cannot drop in on Mark.
   How does Juno respond to Bren's advice?
   What does this tell you about her?

6. Juno tells Bleeker to go out with Katrina De Voort.
   What is she doing here?
   What does this tell you about her?

7. Does Juno have a good sense of humour?
   Give reasons for your answer.

Part Four

Summary

From 59.45 minutes up to 1.14.54 minutes, Spring - Juno driving away

- Part Four is full of action, conflict and confrontation.

- Juno calls Mark from school.

- Juno confronts Bleeker over taking Katrina De Voort to the prom.

- Juno calls to see Mark, who reveals his plan to leave his wife.

- Mark tells Vanessa he is not ready to be a father.

- Juno is very upset by Mark's decision.

Part Four
Cultural Context/Social Setting

Juno's jealousy over Bleeker inviting Katrina De Voort to prom reminds us that despite the many adult decisions Juno has had to make, she lives in a teenage world. Despite her claims that she does not want to go, Juno is clearly hurt that Bleeker is taking another girl to this significant social event.

Mark's plans to leave Vanessa demonstrate how temporary relationships can be in this world. Their marriage will be easily disassembled and each character will move on to live a separate life of their own. Mark has made this decision, there are no obstacles preventing him from going through with it, divorce is perfectly acceptable and available in this world.

Mark is free to opt out of the adult world of parenthood and choose a freer lifestyle for himself.

Questions

1. What do you notice as Juno walks down the school corridor as this part begins?
   What does this tell you?

2. "Pretty much everyone's making fun of me behind my back."
   Can you explain why people are making fun of Juno behind her back?
   How must she be feeling?
   Do you think this is a big problem for her?
   Explain your point of view.

3. "Are you ashamed that we did it? Because at least you don't have to have the evidence under your sweater."
   What stigma is Juno referring to here?
   Is Bleeker treated the same as Juno by their peers?
   Why/why not?

4. What is prom?
   Do you think that it is a big deal that Juno will miss it?
   Give reasons for your answer.

5. Is it easy for Mark to leave his wife?
   Fully explain your point of view.

6. What problems has her pregnancy caused for Juno?
   Be specific in your answer.

7. What does everyday teenage life involve in the world of this film?

8. Has her pregnancy changed Juno's life?
Use examples to support your point of view.

9. What insight does this part give into marriage in this world?
Give reasons for your answer.

10. What is 'adult life' like in this world?
Is it very different to 'teenage life'?

Part Four
Literary Genre

Notice that indie love songs play in the background a lot of the time, lending an upbeat vibe to the text, reminding us that this is a teenage love story.

There is conflict when Juno confronts Bleeker about taking Katrina De Voort to the prom. Juno is mean and cutting, taking out her frustrations on him.

Mark's decision to leave Vanessa provides tension and conflict. He says he expected Juno to be on board with his choice and asks her how she sees him, making us wonder whether there was attraction here, or whether Juno simply helped Mark reconnect with his youth. Either way, she has unknowingly acted as a catalyst in his marriage's breakdown.

Juno did not cry when she discovered she was pregnant, went to the abortion clinic, or when she told her dad and stepmom she was pregnant, but she gets very upset when she learns that Mark and Vanessa are breaking up. Her upset shows how important it is to her that her plan to give her baby to a loving family works out. It also shows how important love is as a theme, this break-up severely affects Juno in a way we have not seen before.

The theme of growing up or embracing adulthood is also seen in this scene. Vanessa tells Mark that his shirt is stupid and to grow up. He is trying to shirk the adult world of responsibilities by leaving Vanessa. This is an important idea, as the theme of accepting adulthood, and being ready for all it involves, is central to the story.

Mark leaving Vanessa introduces uncertainty to the story. It is no longer clear how things will turn out for Juno regarding her baby's adoption, adding tension and suspense to the film.

Questions

1. What is the significance of 'Spring' here?

2. How does the soundtrack add to the tone and mood of this section?

3. How does Juno react to hearing that Bleeker is going to prom with Katrina De Voort?

4. How does the confrontation between Juno and Bleeker over prom add to the story?

5. Juno puts on lipstick before going to see Mark.
   What is being communicated here?
   Have there been any other hints or suggestions along these lines?
   Be specific in your answer.

6. Do you notice anything different about Mark's clothes when Juno calls over?
   Can you explain this change?

7. Comment on the scene where Juno dances with Mark. Why are they dancing?

8. "I'm leaving Vanessa."
   How does Juno react to Mark's bombshell?
   How did he expect her to react?
   Are you surprised by her reaction?
   Give reasons for your answer.

9. How do Mark's plans to leave Vanessa complicate things for Juno?

10. What is the mood like as Juno drives away?

11. Why is Juno so upset?

12. What have you learned about Juno in this section?

13. Did you anticipate or expect a romantic relationship to develop between Juno and Mark?
Why/why not?
Are you happy that Juno is not interested in Mark?
Give a reason for your answer.

14. What is the mood like as this section ends?
What, do you think, will happen next?

15. What makes this an exciting part of the film?
Give reasons for your answer.

Part Four
General Vision and Viewpoint

Juno is hurt to learn that Bleeker is taking Katrina De Voort to the prom, and confronts him about it. He tells her she has no reason to be mad at him, as she broke his heart. This conflict is one of the tenser moments in the text, showing Juno's frustrations and Bleeker's vulnerability.

Mark's plans to leave Vanessa provide one of the darker moments in the text. His failing marriage shows that life is not perfect, and sometimes, dreams do not come true. Juno finds this news particularly upsetting, as it dashes the hopes she had of the perfect adoptive family.

Although he may be perceived as an immature character, for Mark, the break-up is a welcome new beginning. Spending time with Juno has made him realise how controlled his life is, and how he has given up on his own dreams of being in a band. He expects Juno to support this break and his new-found freedom, but instead she is shocked and upset, perhaps even more so than Vanessa.

Juno crying at the roadside is an upsetting moment in the film. Her hopes of placing her baby with a perfect family have been dashed. It is significant that Juno does not cry for long, before gathering herself and driving on. Her ability to calm down and keep going, suggests that hope still lies ahead.

Questions

1. Why is Juno mad at Bleeker?
   Has she a right to be mad at him?
   How does their argument make you feel?
   How does their argument contribute to the general vision and viewpoint?

2. How do Mark's plans to leave Vanessa make you feel?
   Why is Mark leaving Vanessa?
   What do Mark's plans to leave Vanessa suggest about life?

3. How does Vanessa view Mark's hopes of being a rockstar?
   Is she harsh here?
   How does her attitude to Mark's dream colour the general vision and viewpoint here?

4. What do Vanessa and Mark argue and disagree about?

5. What does Mark and Vanessa's argument and the breakdown of their marriage reveal about life?

6. Why does Juno cry at the side of the road?
   How is she feeling here?
   How do you feel at this point in the film?

7. What is the director showing us about life in this part of the film?
   Give reasons for your answer.

Part Four
Relationships

The confrontation between Juno and Bleeker over prom provides an insight into their relationship. Juno says she had sex with Bleeker out of boredom, but he does not believe her. He tells her she broke his heart, and that he should not want to talk to her. She asks if he is ashamed of having sex with her before storming off. Bleeker clearly cares about Juno. Although she does not admit it, Bleeker asking Katrina De Voort to the prom has upset Juno here. Her jealousy suggests that Juno has feelings for Bleeker as she is hurt and angry that he has asked out another girl, even though she suggested it.

Juno and Mark have grown close. They share interests and enjoy chatting together, even dancing in Mark's room. Is is worth considering exactly what the nature of their relationship is. Are they close friends, and is this appropriate in their situation?

Mark is disappointed when Juno reacts negatively to his plans to leave Vanessa. He asks her how she thinks of him and why she calls over. His expectations are not stated explicitly, but he seems to expect more from Juno here. Perhaps he has considered a relationship with Juno? This is hinted at, but not stated overtly. In any case, Mark's relationship with Juno has contributed to his decision to leave his wife.

When Vanessa arrives and sees Juno in tears, she automatically blames Mark for doing something. She assumes he has done something wrong, suggesting a lack of trust or perhaps a willingness to see fault in him.

Mark and Vanessa discuss their divorce in a calm, unemotional way. They do not break down as Juno does. Perhaps they realise, even now, that this is the right decision and that they will be better off when they have separated.

Questions

1. What do you notice about Juno's phonecall to Mark?
   How do you feel about their relationship?

2. According to Juno, why did Bleeker and her have sex?
   What does this tell you about their relationship?

3. Is Juno jealous of Katrina De Voort, do you think?

4. Why does Juno confront Bleeker about prom?
   How is she feeling, do you think?

5. "Your mum must be pretty stoked that you're not taking me."
   Is Bleeker's mother's dislike of Juno a factor in their relationship, do you think?

6. Bleeker asks Juno why she is mad at him.
   What makes her feel this way?
   How would you feel, in her position?

7. How does Juno treat Bleeker during this confrontation?
   Is she fair to him here?
   How does this make you feel?

8. How does Bleeker feel about Juno?
   How does this make you feel?

9. How does this confrontation between Juno and Bleeker add to the theme of relationships?
   Be specific in your answer.

CLASSROOM QUESTIONS • 69

10. When Juno arrives, she asks Mark if Vanessa is home and he repiles, "No, we are safe."
    What does this suggest about Juno and Mark's relationship?
    What does this suggest about Mark and Vanessa's relationship?

11. What is the significance of the comic that Mark gives Juno?

12. Mark tells Juno that he plans to leave Vanessa.
    How does she react?
    What does their conversation reveal about
    a) his relationship with Vanessa and
    b) his relationship with Juno?

13. Vanessa arrives, and seeing Juno in tears, assumes that Mark has done something.
    What does this tell you about her relationship with Mark?

14. What reasons does Mark have for leaving his wife?
    Is he right to leave her, do you think?
    Are Mark and Vanessa upset that their marriage has not worked out?
    What does this tell you about their relationship?
    What does the breakdown of their marriage add to the theme of relationships?

15. What does Juno and Mark's relationship add to the theme of relationships?

Part Four
Hero, Heroine, Villain

Juno is mean to Bleeker when she confronts him about taking Katrina De Voort to prom. Perhaps this is due to frustration over her heavily pregnant state, or jealousy that Bleeker has asked another girl out. In either case, she is unfair in the way she treats him, particularly as she knows how he feels about her.

Juno is very upset by Mark and Vanessa's break-up, showing how much she has invested in them and the happiness they represent. This is the only time we have seen her cry, showing how this break-up has taken its toll on this usually robust and resilient character.

When Mark tells Juno about his plans to leave his wife, he asks her how she sees him. There is the suggestion here that Mark may have read more into their relationship than Juno did. This may show a naivity or lack of experience in her character. We may think of her as more mature and experienced than she actually is, simply because she is pregnant. Bren had warned her that she knew nothing about marriage and that she was inappropriately crossing boundaries, and it seems that, unknownst to Juno, Bren may have been right.

Questions

1. "Why is everyone always staring at me."
   What aspects of her pregnancy is Juno having difficulty with?

2. Why does Juno confront Bleeker about Katrina De Voort?
   Does she treat him fairly here?
   Give reasons for your answer.
   What insight does this confrontation give you into Juno's character and how she is feeling?
   Is she mean to Bleeker here?
   What makes her act this way?
   How would you feel, in her position?

3. Is Juno naive in the scene where Mark tells her his plans to leave Vanessa?
   Give reasons for your answer.

4. Why does Juno want Mark to stay with Vanessa?

5. Why is Juno so upset leaving Mark and Vanessa's?
   What does it tell you about her?
   What does it tell you about how she views her baby?

6. Is Juno finding the adoption process difficult, do you think?
   Give reasons for your answer.

Part Five

Summary

From 1.14.55 minutes to the end, Bleeker playing guitar to end credits

- Mark and Vanessa plan their divorce.
- Juno leaves a note on Vanessa's doorstep.
- Juno talks to her dad about love and listens to his advice.
- Juno apologises to Bleeker and tells him she is in love with him.
- Juno goes into labour.
- Vanessa meets her son.

Part Five
Cultural Context/Social Setting

In the delivery ward, Juno's dad reassures her that she will return there someday, on her own terms. This shows that although this was not the right time for Juno to become a mother, it is still something that her father anticipates in her future.

Juno's whole family go to the hospital with her. They are a cohesive, supportive unit, showing that family is important in the world of the film. They love Juno and are there for her.

Vanessa gets to have her baby, and become a mother. In this world, this is possible without a husband.

Juno returns to her regular, teenage life after having her baby. We see her cycling her bike and playing guitar. The adult world still awaits her in her future.

Questions

1. Will it be easy for Mark and Vanessa to get divorced? Why is this the case?
   What insight into this world does their break-up give you?

2. Mac jokes that he does not approve of Juno dating in her condition.
   What do his comments reveal about the world of this film?

3. What is significant about Juno kissing Bleeker at the running track?
   Fully explain your point of view.

4. What is life like for Juno after giving her baby up for adoption?
   What does this suggest about this world?
   What sort of life do you imagine for her baby?
   Give reasons for your answer.

Part Five
Literary Genre

It is a heart-warming moment when Juno tells Bleeker that she thinks she is in love with him. This is what their relationship has been working towards throughout the film. It resolves the love story in a very positive, feel-good way.

Each of the plotlines are tied together in this final part of the film; Juno has the baby, Vanessa achieves motherhood, and as the film closes, we see that Juno and Bleeker are happy together. Everything has ended well, turning out favourably for the characters. This is a happy, satisfying ending.

Questions

1. Why do we see Bleeker playing his guitar and Juno gazing up at the night sky?
   What is the director showing us here?

2. We don't see what Juno leaves at Mark and Vanessa's door.
   What is the effect of this?
   What do you think it could be?

3. What does Juno's chat with her dad add to the story?
   Be specific in your answer.

4. Juno tells Bleeker that she loves him.
   What does this add to the story?

5. What does Bleeker running to the hospital add to the story?

6. Are the hospital scenes very emotional?
   Explain your point of view.
   How would you expect an audience to feel, watching this section?

7. What did Juno's note to Vanessa say?
   What makes this a powerful message?

8. What is the impact of the 'Summer' section on the storyline?

9. How does the film end?
   Is this a good ending?
   Is this a happy ending?
   Is this a satisfying ending?
   Give reasons to support your point of view.

10. Comment on the song Juno and Bleeker sing at the end.
    How does it contribute to the mood here?
    What message does it give?
    How does it add to the ending?

Part Five
General Vision and Viewpoint

Juno is upset as she wonders whether it is possible for people in love to stay happy forever. Mark's plans to leave Vanessa have shaken her belief in lasting love. Her dad reassures her, saying that he and Bren are very happy together. His sharing of his experience re-affirms Juno's belief in love and encourages her to tell Bleeker how she feels about him.

It is a very positive, uplifting moment when Juno tells Bleeker she is in love with him, and kisses him at the running track. It is heart-warming to see their relationship develop this way.

The ending, although happy, is tinged with sadness. Seeing Juno crying after her baby's delivery shows that this was not an easy process for her to go through.

Overall, the ending is happy, optimistic and forward looking. Vanessa has achieved her dream of being a mother, life has returned to normal for Juno and Bleeker, and as a young couple in love, their lives are full of potential. This is an uplifting, hopeful end to the film.

Questions

1. Are Mark and Vanessa upset to be getting divorced?

2. What is Vanessa most upset about?

3. How does Mark feel about leaving his wife?
   What does Mark and Vanessa's outlook suggest about their relationship?
   What does Mark and Vanessa's outlook suggest about life?
   Do you find their break-up upsetting? Why/why not?

4. "I need to know that it's possible that two people can stay happy together forever."
   Is this the film's message?
   Give reasons for your answer.

5. Juno's dad says he is very happy with Bren.
   How does this happiness contribute to the general vision and viewpoint here?

6. What advice does Mac give Juno?
   Is this good advice?
   How does this advice impact on the general vision and viewpoint?

7. How do you feel when Juno tells Bleeker she is in love with him?

8. "Every time I see you, the baby starts kicking super hard."
   Is this happy or sad?
   Explain your viewpoint.

9. Juno's whole family go with her to the hospital.
   What is significant about this?
   How does it make you feel?

10. When Bleeker sees that Juno is not at his race, he runs to the hospital.
    How does this make you feel?

11. Juno's dad tells her that someday she will be back in the maternity ward, on her own terms.
    How does this affect the film's outlook?

12. What is the mood like when Bleeker arrives in the hospital?
    How does seeing him comfort Juno make you feel?

13. Juno and Bleeker decide not to see the baby.
    How does this make you feel?

14. Why might someone cry at this part of the film?
    Be specific in your answer.

15. How do you feel watching Vanessa hold her son for the first time?

16. How does Vanessa achieving her wish to be a mother impact on the general vision and viewpoint of the film?

17. What significant details do you notice in the 'Summer' section?
What is the director telling us here?
How does this make you feel?

18. How does Juno feel about Bleeker as the film ends?
How does this affect the general vision and viewpoint?

19. Will Juno and Bleeker be happy do you think?
Explain your point of view.
Will Vanessa and her baby be happy do you think?
Explain your point of view.
How does the future happiness of characters impact on the general vision and viewpoint as the story ends?
Explain your point of view.

20. How do you feel as the film ends?
What makes you feel this way?

Part Five
Relationships

Juno's chat with her dad shows the positive relationships in the film. Her dad realises something is bothering her, and reassures her, showing how he understands and cares about his daughter. This chat also makes Juno realise how much Bleeker cares about her, and she him, further adding to the theme of relationships.

Juno tells Bleeker that she is in love with him, and kisses him at the running track. This is what their relationship has been building towards. Juno and Bleeker are finally together.

Juno's whole family, and her friend Leah, go to the hospital with her, showing how they support and care about her.

Bleeker runs to the hospital to be with Juno after the baby's birth. Clearly, he cares a lot about her and realises how difficult this is for her.

The final image of Juno and Bleeker singing together is very positive. They are presented as a young couple, very much in love.

Overall, relationships in this film are generally warm, positive and supportive, bringing happiness and love to the film's characters. Where there are conflicts between characters, they are resolved positively.

Questions

1. Are Mark and Vanessa upset to be getting divorced?
   Why, do you think, is this the case?

2. Does Juno's dad know her well?

3. "I think I've found that person."
   What does chatting with her dad make Juno realise?

4. Why does Juno go to see Bleeker at the track?
   Did you expect this development?
   Give reasons for your answer.

5. Bren and Leah are with Juno during labour.
   What does this tell you about relationships in this film?

6. Bleeker runs straight to the hospital when he realises Juno has missed his race.
   How does Bleeker feel about Juno?

7. Juno gives Vanessa her baby, knowing that Mark has left her.
   What does this tell you about how Juno views Vanessa?

8. How does Juno feel about Bleeker as the film ends?
   How has their relationship changed over the course of the film?
   Do they have a good relationship?
   Give reasons for your answer.

Part Five
Hero, Heroine, Villain

Juno is very upset by Mark and Vanessa's break-up as it shakes her belief in love's ability to last. This shows how important this is to her.

Juno realises that she is in love with Bleeker, and goes and tells him.

Juno goes through with the adoption, as promised. Her tears in the hospital show how upset she is, as perhaps does her decision not to see the baby. She has followed through on the kind act she promised from the moment when she decided to have the baby.

As the film ends, Juno is a regular teenager again. Her life has returned to normal. She looks happy and content as she sings with Bleeker in the final scene.

Questions

1. What does Juno's chat with her dad tell you about her?
   What worries does she have?
   What does she want to believe?
   What does she want from life?

2. Are you happy for Juno when she kisses Bleeker?
   Give reasons for your answer.

3. After the baby is born, how does Juno feel about giving him up for adoption, do you think?

4. Is Juno a childish or mature character?
   Give reasons for your answer.

5. Does Juno cope well with her unplanned pregnancy?
   Give reasons for your answer.

6. Is Juno a regular teenager?
   Fully explain your point of view, using examples to support your ideas.

7. Is Juno a likeable character?
   Give reasons for your answer.

8. Is Juno a relatable character?
   Give reasons for your answer.

The Comparative Study

Cultural Context/Social Setting

*Cultural Context/Social Setting refers to the world of the text.
Consider social norms, beliefs, values and attitudes.*

Juno is a modern day teenager who discovers she is pregnant. Initially she decides to have an abortion, before changing her mind and opting to privately adopt the baby instead. This is a world where Juno is free to make these choices.

Juno's world is a generally loving and supportive place. Her family are very supportive of her, as are Bleeker and Leah. She is not isolated by her predicament, having people to rely on.

Juno refers to people talking about her behind her back, but the judgements of others are given to us in a second hand way. We do not see Juno being mocked or judged for being pregnant, with the exception of the ultrasound episode, where Bren jumps to her defence. Juno's pregnancy is portrayed as an inconvenience, not as something that will determine the rest of her life or her position in society.

Vanessa is clearly wealthy and successful in her career. However, she chooses to become a mother. This shows that women are free to choose what kind of lives they want to live in this world. Just as Juno can choose not to be a parent, Vanessa can choose to become one.

Men, in this text, (Mac, Bleeker, Mark) are shown to be kind and supportive.

Juno has positive relationships with each of these male characters where she is understood and valued, adding to the sense that this is a positive, supportive world.

1. Describe the store clerk's attitude to Juno's positive pregnancy test.
   What does this tell you about the world of the film?

2. What does Juno decide to do about her pregnancy at first?
   Can you explain this decision?
   What does it tell you about the world of the text?

3. How do Leah, Juno's dad and stepmom, and Bleeker, respond to the news of Juno's pregnancy?
   What do their responses reveal about their world?

4. How do characters view Juno because she is pregnant?
   Be specific in your answer.
   What does this tell you about this world?

5. Why won't Vanessa have a baby shower?
   What does this tell you about her friends' attitude to the adoption?

6. "Mark is a married man. There are boundaries."
   Why is Brenda concerned about Juno visiting Mark?
   What insight does this give you into this world?

7. Bleeker's parents do not know that he is the father of Juno's baby.
   What does this tell you about this world?

8. What does the setting of the film tell you about the world of the characters?
Be specific in your answer.

9. What does this film suggest about adulthood and maturity?
Give reasons for your answer.

10. What is the role of women in the world of this film?

11. What is the role of men in the world of this film?

12. Vanessa chooses to be a mother, rather than devoting herself to her career.
What does this tell you about this world?

13. Juno is presented as a confident, intelligent, capable teenager.
What does this suggest to you about this world?

14. Are money and wealth important in this world?
Are school and academia important in this world?
What is valued in the world of this film?
What does this tell you about this place?

15. Is this a judgemental world?
Explain your point of view.

16. What strikes you most about the world of this film?
Give reasons for your answer.

Literary Genre

Literary Genre refers to the way the story is told. Consider aspects of narration such as the manner and style of narration, characterisation, setting, tension, literary techniques, etc.

Character

Juno is a strong, independent lead character, forced to make very demanding adult decisions. Her optimism, humour, honesty and kindness make her very likeable and relatable.

Juno's humour and optimism colour the story. Her resilience and upbeat personality influence the tone of the film, making it bright, positive and sunny.

Humour

Humour in any text provides light relief and entertainment. It works very well in 'Juno' in the following ways:

1) Humour adds to how we feel about the characters, making them more likeable. We enjoy Juno's wisecracks and quirky comments, humour endears her to us.
2) Humour is used at key points in the film to relieve tension. For example, during Juno's confrontation with Bleeker, she accuses his 'girlfriend' of giving her the 'stink eye', to which Bleeker replies that that is just her face. His sincere response is very funny, relieving some of the tension and preventing the scene from being too harsh or heated.

3) Reassurance - at times the use of humour reassures the audience that everything will turn out okay. For example, at Juno's ultrasound, and when Vanessa meets her son, Bren's honest, straight-talking is funny, offering relief to the tension in these scenes.

Soundtrack

The soundtrack helps to set the tone of the film. Much of the time, indie lovesongs play in the background, feeding into the film's love story. The soundtrack also helps demonstrate the teenage world of the text.

Tension

In the film's early stages there is tension around Juno's pregnancy. Telling her dad and stepmom is a tense moment for Juno, as she fears how they will react.

Most of the film's tension revolves around Mark's decision to leave Vanessa. This means that the adoption may not go through, making Juno and Vanessa's futures uncertain. It also involves the audience emotionally in the action, as we wonder what will happen next and how this problem will be resolved.

Conflict

We see conflict in the scene where Juno confronts Bleeker over his prom date with Katrina De Voort. While she is cutting and mean in what she says to him, Bleeker says that she broke his heart. This is an emotional scene that makes the story's outcome uncertain, further engaging the audience's interest.

Interestingly, there is no villain in this film. Characters are warm and positive. Conflict appears in obstacles that must be overcome, rather than negative characters.

1. How is this story told? (Consider the film format)
   Why is the story told in this way?
   What is the effect of this?

2. How does the film's opening arouse your interest and curiosity?

3. What are your first impressions of Juno?
   How does Juno react to the positive pregnancy test?
   What does this tell you about her character?
   Does your view of her change during the film?
   Explain your point of view.

4. What are your first impressions of Paulie Bleeker?
   Does your view of him change during the film?

5. What makes it tense when Juno tells her dad and stepmom that she is pregnant?
   Be specific in your answer.

6. How does Juno's first meeting with Mark and Vanessa go?

7. How do you get a sense of Mark and Vanessa's wealth?

8. Do Juno and Mark get on well?
   How is this established?
   What are you expecting to happen next?

9. What is your response to seeing Juno spend time with Mark?
   What does this add to the story?

10. What does Juno seeing Vanessa in the mall add to the story?

11. Is it a tense moment in the film when Mark tells Juno his plans to leave Vanessa?
If so, what makes it tense?
Did you anticipate this development?
Did Juno anticipate this development?
How do Mark's plans, and Juno's response to this news, add to the story?

12. What makes the scene where Mark backs out of the adoption dramatic?
Be specific in your answer.

13. What makes us invest ourselves emotionally in the love story in this film?

14. Is Juno's character likeable?
Give reasons for your answer.
Is Juno's character relatable?
Give reasons for your answer.
How does Juno's character grow and develop over the course of the film?
Give reasons for your answer.

15. Juno is a confident, intelligent teenager.
How does her character aid the storytelling in this film?

16. What obstacles is Juno met with over the course of the film?

How well does she deal with these difficulties?
Include examples in your answer.

17. Is Juno an adult or a child?
What makes you say this?
How does this aspect of her character add to the storytelling?

18. Is Juno a good lead character?
Explain your point of view.

19. Is there humour in this film?
How does it add to the story?

20. Is this a 'feel-good' movie?
How does it fit this label?
Be specific in your answer.

21. Is the issue of teenage pregnancy handled well in this film?
Give a reason for your answer.
Is it treated seriously?
Is it treated positively or negatively?
Be specific in your answer.
What does the director choose to focus on?
How does this shape the story?
What comment, if any, is he making about modern life?

22. Is the issue of adoption handled well in this film?
Is it treated seriously?
Is it treated positively or negatively?
Be specific in your answer.

23. Does this film have a happy ending?
What makes it happy/unhappy?
Be specific in your answer.
Is it a satisfying ending?
Explain your point of view.

24. Do you think the cast of this film are well chosen?
Explain your point of view.
How do the actors enhance and add to the way the story is told?

25. What music is used in the soundtrack?
How does the soundtrack add to the storytelling?

26. How does seeing and hearing the characters add to the storytelling?

27. Is this a very visual text?
How does it compare with your other texts in this regard?
How does this impact on your enjoyment of the story?

28. Comment on the mood as the story ends.

29. Where does this story take place?
How does setting contribute to the story?

30. Do you find this film to be interesting and easy to follow?
What draws the audience into this story?
Highlight specific aspects of the text in your answer.

31. How does the author create a bright, sunny feel to the story?

32. Where do you see conflict in this story?
How does the use of conflict add to this story?

33. Is this a realistic story?
Support your view.

34. Are there fairytale elements in this story?
Give reasons for your answer.

35. Is this story predictable?
Did you expect Juno to make the choices she does?

36. Did you enjoy this story?
Use examples from the text to support your answer.

37. Who is your favourite character in this film?
What makes you like/admire them?

38. Who is your least favourite character in this film?
What makes you dislike them?

39. What themes can you identify in this story?

40. Is this film about choices?
Explain your view.

41. How might 'Juno' be considered to be a coming-of-age movie?

42. The New York Times said the film had an underlying message that "is not anti-abortion but rather pro-adulthood."

Do you agree with this interpretation of the film?
Give reasons for your answer.

43. In its review, 'Empire' called 'Juno' "a sharp-edged, sweet-centred, warm-hearted coming of age movie that's always just that little bit smarter than you think it is."
Do you agree with these comments?
Give reasons for your answer.

General Vision and Viewpoint

General Vision and Viewpoint refers to the author's outlook or view of life and how this viewpoint is represented in the text.

Overall, Juno is a very positive text. Juno deals with her pregnancy maturely, planning to give her baby to a good family as she realises she is not yet ready for motherhood. She tells her family her plans, and they support her. She is supported and cared for throughout the film.

The love story that develops between Juno and Bleeker is also very positive and optimistic. They begin as best friends, and end the film as a young couple who have been through a lot together and have a future full of potential and possibility.

Vanessa adopting Juno's baby is another very positive aspect of the film. She says she was born to be a mother, and thanks to Juno, she gets to realise this dream. This is very positive, as both Juno and Vanessa can be happy in the future.

Mark leaving Vanessa to pursue his dream of being a rockstar may appear selfish, childish and immature. However, his dream is very hopeful and optimisitc. Also, Vanessa does not appear to be very upset by the break-up, limiting the impact it has on darkening the general vision and viewpoint.

1. Does Juno cope well when she discovers her unplanned pregnancy?
   How does her attitude affect the mood of the film?

2. How does Bleeker react to Juno's pregnancy?
   Why does he react this way?
   What does she plan to do about it?

3. Is her adoption plan a positive or negative development?

4. Juno's dad and stepmom are very supportive of her and her decision to have the baby adopted.
   How does this add to the film's outlook?

5. Juno does not want to 'sell' her baby, she just wants it to be with people who will love it and be good parents.
   How does Juno's motivation here contribute to the general vision and viewpoint?
   Would things be different if she wished to be paid to give her baby up?
   Explain your view.

6. Vanessa tells Juno that she is doing a beautiful and selfless thing for them.
   Is this true, do you think?
   What does this suggest about human nature and life?

7. What impact has meeting Juno made on Mark and Vanessa's lives?
   Is this a positive or negative development?

8. How is Juno perceived by others because she is pregnant?
   How does this make you feel?
   What does this tell you about people?

9. How do you feel when Juno encourages Bleeker to go out with Katrina De Voort?
   Why, do you think, does she do this?

10. What is the atmosphere like when Juno confronts Bleeker about taking Katrina De Voort to prom?
    How does she treat him here?
    Why does she act this way?
    How does this moment contribute to the film's general vision and viewpoint?
    How does this moment make you feel?

11. How does Mark leaving Vanessa affect the mood of the film at this point?

12. Why is Juno so upset when she pulls over onto the hard shoulder?
    How does her future look?
    Should she be so upset, in your view?

13. Is Mark and Vanessa's break-up upsetting?
    Why/why not?

14. Why does Vanessa's relationship with Mark fail?
    Could it have been succesful, in this world?
    Will this break-up bring them happiness or sorrow, in your view?

How does this contribute to the general vision and viewpoint of the film?

15. "I need to know that it's possible that two people can stay happy together forever."
    Is this what this film is about?
    Is this a hopeful or hopeless notion?

16. Juno's dad tells her to find someone who loves her for exactly what she is.
    What is your response to this advice?
    Is this a positive message?

17. How do you feel when Bleeker checks his mailbox?

18. "I think I'm in love with you."
    How does Juno's statement here affect the film's mood?

19. "Every time I see you the baby starts kicking super hard."
    Comment on this.
    Is this a happy or sad moment in the film?

20. Juno's stepmother and best friend are with her during her labour.
    What does this add to the story's message?

21. Are the scenes in the hospital sad?
    Explain your view.
    What do they suggest about life?

22. "He didn't feel like ours. I think he was always hers."
    How do Juno's words here make you feel?

23. Do characters in this film have opportunities and the potential for happiness?
How does this add to the film's outlook?
What does it suggest about life?

24. Juno follows through with her promise to Vanessa, and gives her her baby, without Mark being part of the picture.
What is the director revealing about human nature and life here?

25. What do Juno's experiences show you about people and life?

26. As the film ends, do you feel optimistic about Juno and Bleeker's future?
Give a reason for your answer.

27. Are you happy with how things have turned out?

28. Does Juno have an optimisitic, hopeful approach to life?
Do the other characters share this approach to life?
What does this behaviour suggest about life?

29. Where do you see happiness in this film?
Where do you see sadness in this film?
Which is a greater force in this film?
Fully explain you point of view.

30. Is love sure to succeed in this world?
Explain your point of view.

31. Are characters in this text hopeful and forward looking about life?
Are they realistic? Do they make well-thought out plans?
What does this suggest about their outlook in life?

32. What does this film suggest about human nature?
Is this outlook positive or negative?

33. Is there a lesson or moral to this story?
What could it be?

34. Does the film end on a hopeful or hopeless note?

35. Is life to be enjoyed or endured in the world of this text?
Refer to the film to support your ideas.
Explain your point of view.

36. Is life perfect in this film?
Use examples to support your view.

37. What is the message behind this film?
What is the director, Jason Reitman, telling us about life in this story?
Is this an encouraging, uplifting or depressing outlook?
Give reasons for your answer.

Theme/Issue
Relationships

Relationships has been selected as the theme/issue to explore in relation to this text.

The theme of relationships can be applied to any relationship in a text and includes love, marriage, friendship and family bonds. Consider the complexities of relationships and the impact they have on characters' lives.

The relationships in Juno are very positive. Characters are honest, open and kind to one another. Juno's father and stepmom are very happy together, an example of lasting love. Juno and Bleeker care about each other throughout the film, and are happy together as the film ends. Leah and Juno have a strong friendship and Leah is a loyal friend.

On a more negative note, Mark leaves Vanessa as the pressure and adult demands of becoming a father are too much for him. However, Mark and Vanessa can discusss their divorce together, without tears or arguments. Their relationship ends in a very low-key, amicable way, with Vanessa still getting to achieve her dream of becoming a mother. Their split does not impact on their potential for future happiness.

Although an inappropriate relationship between Juno and Mark is hinted at, they are never anything more than friends. He asks her how she sees him, but there is never anything predatory in his behaviour. It may be that Mark seeks a connection with his youth, rather than a connection with Juno.

1. What are your first impressions of the teenagers' relationship?

2. How does Bleeker feel about Juno in the early stages of the film?
Use examples to support your view.

3. How does Juno react when she hears that Bleeker is going to prom with Katrina De Voort?
What is your response to this?

4. When Juno confronts Bleeker over Katrina De Voort, he tells her that she broke his heart.
Describe their relationship at this point.

5. Are Juno and Bleeker good friends?
Does this help their relationship?

6. What strengths do you see in Juno and Bleeker's relationship?

7. What weaknesses or problems do you see in Juno and Bleeker's relationship?

8. What complicates Juno and Bleeker's relationship?

9. Are Juno and Bleeker a good match?
Explain your view.

10. How does Juno and Bleeker's relationship change and develop over the course of the story?

11. Is this a positive or negative relationship?

12. Does Juno have a good relationship with her mother?

13. "You're looking a little morose honey."
    Does Juno's dad understand her well?

14. "I'll always be there to love you and support you no matter what kind of pickle you're in."
    Does Juno's dad love and support her?
    Use examples to support your ideas.

15. When Juno goes into labour, she calls for her dad. Comment on this.

16. Does Juno have a good relationship with her father, Mac?

17. Does Juno have a good relationship with her stepmom, Brenda?

18. How does Bleeker's mom's dislike of Juno impact on Juno and Bleeker's relationship?
    Give reasons for your answer.

19. Does Bleeker have a good relationship with his parents?
    Use examples to support your view.

20. Do Mark and Vanessa have a good relationship?
    Explain your view.

21. Do Mac and Bren have a good relationship?
    Explain your view.

22. Do Juno and her friend Leah have a good relationship?
    Explain your view.

23. Do you think Juno would have coped as well with her pregnancy and the adoption without the support of her family and friends?
Give reasons for your answer.

24. Overall, are relationships generally positive or negative in the film?
Use examples to support your view.

Hero, Heroine, Villain

'Hero, Heroine, Villain' refers to studying central characters (protagonists/antagonists).

Their traits, values, etc. and their ability to deal with conflict, challenges, obstacles, etc. should be considered.

Juno McGuff

Juno is a very likeable character. She is funny and entertaining to watch, and genuine and sincere in how she treats people.

She copes well with her unplanned pregnancy, choosing to have her baby adopted by a family that really want and need it. This is a very positive, brave outlook to have.

Her need to believe in love shows her optimistic, hopeful outlook.

Juno is confident and independent, making important choices and decisions for herself. She shows strength and resilience in the way she copes and deals with her unplanned pregnancy.

1. What are your first impressions of Juno as the film begins?
   How does your view of her develop throughout the story?

2. How well does she cope with her pregnancy?
   What is your response to this?

3. Why does she choose to give her baby up for adoption?
   What is your response to this?

4. Early in the film, Juno tells her father she doesn't know what kind of girl she is.
   What does this tell you about her?
   Do you think this is usual for a sixteen year old?

5. Is Juno a likeable character?
   Give reasons for your answer.

6. Is Juno a relatable character?
   Give reasons for your answer.

7. Is Juno selfish and self-centred or kind and generous?
   Is she naive and innocent or wise and wordly?
   Refer to the text to support the points you make.

8. What sort of life has Juno had?
   How has this affected her as a person?

9. Is Juno faced with a lot of challenges and problems in the film?
   How does she deal with these challenges and problems?
   What is your response to this?

10. Does Juno grow and develop over the course of the film? Give reasons for your answer.

11. Do you like Juno McGuff? What makes you feel this way about her?

The Comparative Study: Comparing Texts

Use the following questions to compare your texts, noting the similarities and differences between them. Include examples to support the points that you make.

Cultural Context/Social Setting

Consider each of your chosen texts in your answers.

1. In which of the texts you have studied for the Comparative Study do characters have the most freedom and choice?
   Why is this the case?
   Justify your answer with examples from your chosen texts.

2. In which of your texts are characters most controlled?

3. Who holds the power in each world?
   Who is powerless?

4. In which world is difference most accepted and respected?
   In which world is difference least accepted and respected?

5. Which world is the least tolerant?
   Which world is the most tolerant?
   Include examples to explain your view.

6. Which world is the best to live in if you are a woman?
   Give reasons for your answer.

7. Which world is the best to live in if you are a man?
   Give reasons for your answer.

8. Which world is the best to live in if you are a child?
   Give reasons for your answer.

9. Which text portrays the most violent and volatile world?

10. Which of your texts portrays the safest, most secure place?

11. Which of your texts portrays the most supportive world?

12. Which of these worlds is the darkest, most fearful place?

13. Which of these worlds is the brightest, most joyful place?

14. Which of these places is the most unpredictable?

15. Which text portrays the most traditional world?

16. Which of these societies holds family in the highest esteem?

17. Which of these societies holds love in the highest esteem?
    Which of these societies holds love in the lowest esteem?

18. Which of these societies holds religion in the highest esteem?
    Which of these societies holds religion in the lowest esteem?

19. Which of these societies holds power in the highest esteem?

20. Which of these societies holds wealth in the highest esteem?

21. Where do you see the best treatment of the vulnerable of society? Include examples to support your view.

22. Where do you see the worst treatment of the vulnerable of society? Include examples to support your view.

23. Which of the worlds you have studied is the most materialistic?
    Which of the worlds you have studied is the least materialistic?
    What makes characters have these outlooks?

24. Which of the worlds you have studied is the most secretive?
    What makes characters behave this way?

25. Which of your texts displays the greediest world?
    What makes characters have this attitude?

26. Where is love most important?
    Where is love most successful?

Where is love least important?
Where is love least succesful?
Compare the success of love in each of your chosen texts. What does this tell you about the worlds of these texts and characters' lives?

27. Which of these worlds appealed to you most?
Give reasons for your answer.

28. Which of these worlds appealed to you least?
Explain your point of view.

29. Which of your texts is home to the most religious or spiritual world?

30. Which of your texts showed the least religious or spiritual society?

31. How important is social class in each of your texts?

32. In which of your texts are characters most accepting of their world and society?

33. In which of your texts do characters challenge their world, society and values most?

34. In which of your texts do you see the greatest inequality?

35. In which of your texts do you see the greatest injustice?

36. Where do characters behave the best towards one another?

How does Cultural Context/Social Setting influence their behaviour?

37. How do characters reflect the Cultural Context/Social Setting of their worlds?
Explain, including examples.

38. How does the Cultural Context/Social Setting of your texts lead to problems and difficulties for the texts' characters?
How does it affect characters' responses to these difficulties?

39. Which key moments best capture the Cultural Context/Social Setting of each of your texts?

40. What similarities do you notice in the Cultural Context/Social Setting of this text and your other Comparative Study texts?

41. What differences do you notice in the Cultural Context/Social Setting of this text and your other Comparative Study texts?

Literary Genre

1. Did you like the way this story was told more than your other Comparative Study texts?
   State what you enjoyed most (and least) about each.

2. Is this text more exciting than your other texts?
   Consider tension, suspense, pacing, conflict and the author's use of the unexpected.

3. How does the author make use of tension in each of your chosen texts?
   Where is it most effective?
   Where is it least effective?
   Use examples to support your point of view.

4. How does the author make use of climax in each of your chosen texts?
   Where is it most effective?
   Where is it least effective?
   Use examples to support your point of view.

5. How does the author make use of resolution in each of your chosen texts?
   Where is it most effective?
   Where is it least effective?
   Use examples to support your point of view.

6. Are characters more engaging in this text than in your other texts?
Refer to each of your texts in your answer.

7. How does the author create vivid, memorable characters in each of your chosen texts?

8. In which of your texts are characters most life-like and compelling?
In which text are characters least life-like and most difficult to relate to?
Refer to each of your texts in your answer.

9. Is the setting more effective in telling the story in this text, than in your other texts?

10. Is this text more unpredictable than your other texts?
Refer to each of your texts in your answer.

11. Does this text have greater emotional power than your other texts?
Was this emotional power created in a more interesting way here or in a different text?
Refer to each of your texts in your answer.

12. What was your favourite literary technique, used by the author of each of your texts?
How did the use of this technique help the storytelling?

13. To what extent are you influenced by the point of view that this story is told from?
Are you influenced to a greater or lesser degree by the

point of view utilised in your other Comparative Study texts?

14. Which key moments best capture Literary Genre in each of your texts?

15. What similarities do you notice in the Literary Genre of this text and your other Comparative Study texts? Mention specific aspects of narrative.

16. What differences do you notice in the Literary Genre of this text and your other Comparative Study texts? Mention specific aspects of narrative.

General Vision and Viewpoint

1. Is life happier and fuller for characters in this text than in your other Comparative Study texts?
Explain your point of view fully.

2. Do characters in this text face more obstacles and difficulties than in your other texts?
Who struggles most?

3. Are characters in this text rewarded more for their struggles than in your other texts?
Do they overcome adversity and achieve true happiness and contentment in a way that is not realised in your other texts?

4. How do events in these texts, and your personal response to these events, help your understanding of the General Vision and Viewpoint of these texts?
Include specific examples in your answer.

5. How does your attitude to central characters help shape your understanding of the General Vision and Viewpoint of your chosen texts?
Include specific reference to your chosen characters in your answer.

6. What aspects of this text did you respond to emotionally? How does this help your understanding of the General Vision and Viewpoint of the text?
How does this compare to your other texts?

7. Is this the brightest, most hopeful and triumphant text you have studied?
Explain why its message is more or less positive than in your other texts.

8. Which of your chosen texts was the bleakest and most upsetting or depressing?
Explain what made it more negative than your other texts. What made them more positive?

9. Plot your three texts on a scale of one to ten from darkest (most pessimistic) to brightest (most optimistic). Add a note to explain their positions.

10. Which key moments best capture the General Vision and Viewpoint of each of your texts?

11. What similarities do you notice in the General Vision and Viewpoint of this text and your other Comparative Study texts?

12. What differences do you notice in the General Vision and Viewpoint of this text and your other Comparative Study texts?

13. Can you relate any aspect of this text to your own life experience?
    If so, how does this help to shape your understanding of the General Vision and Viewpoint of this text?

Theme/Issue - Relationships

1. Are relationships in this text more positive and supportive than the relationships in your other chosen texts?
   Include specific examples in your answer.

2. Rank the relationships you have studied in your various texts from most positive (score of 10) to most negative (score of 1).
   Add a note explaining your choices.

3. Are relationships in this text the most engaging and interesting that you have studied?
   Explain your choice.

4. Rank the relationships you have studied in your various texts from the most interesting (score of 10) to the least interesting (score of 1).
Add a note explaining your choices.

5. Did you learn most about the theme of relationships from this text or another text on your Comparative Study course?
Refer to your chosen texts to support your answer.

6. What similarities do you notice in the theme of relationships in this text and your other Comparative Study texts?

7. What differences do you notice in the theme of relationships in this text and your other Comparative Study texts?

8. How do the events of the text impact on the characters' relationships with one another in this text and your other chosen texts?
Who is most affected?
Who is least affected?

9. How does conflict impact on the relationships of characters in this text and your other chosen texts?
Who is most affected?
Who is least affected?

10. How does social class impact on the relationships of characters in this text and your other chosen texts?

Who is most affected?
Who is least affected?

11. Is the theme of relationships portrayed in an idealistic or realistic way in each of your chosen texts?

12. Did any aspect of the theme of relationships shock or surprise you in your three chosen texts?
Use examples from your texts to support the points that you make.

13. What are the most interesting aspects of the theme of relationships in each of your chosen texts?

14. Which text taught you most about relationships?
Refer to each text in your answer.

15. Which key moments best capture the theme of relationships in each of your texts?

16. What similarities do you notice in the theme of relationships in this text and your other Comparative Study texts?

17. What differences do you notice in the theme of relationships in this text and your other Comparative Study texts?

Hero/Heroine/Villain

Consider the following list of questions for a central character in each of your chosen texts.

1. Who is the most interesting character in the text?
   What makes them interesting?
   What do you like about them?
   What do you dislike about them?
   What are this character's strengths?
   What are this character's weaknesses?

2. How does this character cope with conflict?

3. How does this character cope with the unexpected?

4. Are they a resourceful character?

5. Are they an emotional character?
   Use examples to support your view.

6. Do you empathise with this character? Why/why not?

7. What do you admire about this character?

8. How well does this character relate to and interact with other characters?
   Include examples to support your points.

9. Is this character happy or sad?

10. Are they an active or passive character?
    How do they contribute to the action and storyline of the text?
    Are they important to the story's plot and development?

11. Is this character a good (successful and interesting) main character?

12. Would you like to meet this character?
    If you met them, what would you talk about?

13. If you had any advice for this character, what would it be?

14. Does this character make the story more exciting?
    In what way do they do this?

15. Is this character a hero/heroine or a villain?
    Explain your choice.

16. Identify the key moments in the text that illustrate your chosen character's personality traits/character.

17. On a scale of one to ten (with one being extremely heroic and ten being an evil villain), where would you place your chosen character?
    Give reasons for your choice.
    Where would you place the main characters from your other texts?
    Why would you place them here?

18. Which of your chosen characters do you like and admire most?

What makes them your favourite character?
Give reasons for your answer.

19. Which of your chosen characters do you dislike most?
Explain why you like some more than others.

20. Which of your chosen characters shocked you most?
Give reasons for your answer.

21. Which of your chosen characters impressed you most?
Give reasons for your answer.

22. Which of your chosen characters did you feel most sorry for?
Give reasons for your answer.

23. Who is the most resourceful character you have come across?
Give reasons for your answer.

24. Which of your chosen characters faced the most problems and difficulties?
Did they cope well with these problems?

25. How is your favourite character similar to the characters in your other texts?

26. How is your favourite character different to the characters in your other texts?

27. Choose key moments from each of your texts to highlight your characters' strengths and weaknesses.

www.ingramcontent.com/pod-product-compliance
Lightning Source LLC
Chambersburg PA
CBHW070951080526
44587CB00015B/2259